MAKERS

LALA YOUSAFZAI

Nobel Peace Prize Winner and Education Activist

by Andrea Wang

Content Consultant
Anita Weiss, Professor and Head, Department of
International Studies, University of Oregon

Core Library

An Imprint of Abdo Publishing
www.abdopublishing.com

www.abdopublishing.com

Published by Abdo Publishing, a division of ABDO, PO Box 398166, Minneapolis, Minnesota 55439. Copyright © 2015 by Abdo Consulting Group, Inc. International copyrights reserved in all countries. No part of this book may be reproduced in any form without written permission from the publisher. Core Library™ is a trademark and logo of Abdo Publishing.

Printed in the United States of America, North Mankato, Minnesota
092014
012015

Cover Photo: Craig Ruttle/AP Images
Interior Photos: Craig Ruttle/AP Images, 1; Anja Niedringhaus/AP Images, 4, 16; Haseeb Ali/epa/Corbis, 8; Christophe Boisvieux/age fotostock/SuperStock, 10; Rainer Lesniewski/ Shutterstock Images, 12; Colin Mcconnell/The Toronto Star/Corbis, 15; Jessica Rinaldi/ AP Images, 18, 45; Kamran Jebrelli/AP Images, 21; B. K. Bangash/AP Images, 24; Red Line Editorial, 26; Naveed Ali/AP Images, 30; University Hospitals Birmingham NHS Foundation Trust/AP Images, 32; Arshad Arbab/Corbis, 34; Mary Altaffer/AP Images, 36; Yui Mok/AP Images, 39; Rui Vieira/Press Association/AP Images, 40

Editor: Arnold Ringstad
Series Designer: Becky Daum

Library of Congress Control Number: 2014944252

Cataloging-in-Publication Data
Wang, Andrea.
 Malala Yousafzai: Nobel Peace Prize winner and education activist / Andrea Wang.
  p. cm. -- (Newsmakers)
Includes bibliographical references and index.
ISBN 978-1-62403-646-0
1. Yousafzai, Malala, 1997- --Juvenile literature. 2. Youth--Political activity--Pakistan--Biography--Juvenile literature. 3. Social justice--Pakistan--Biography--Juvenile literature. 4. Social justice--Study and teaching--Juvenile literature.
1.Title.
371.822095491--dc23
[B]
                                                        2014944252

CONTENTS

CHAPTER ONE
No Ordinary Day 4

CHAPTER TWO
Born a Poor Girl 10

CHAPTER THREE
Becoming an Activist 18

CHAPTER FOUR
Becoming a Target 24

CHAPTER FIVE
The World Listens to Malala . . 34

Important Dates 42

Stop and Think 44

Glossary 46

Learn More 47

Index 48

About the Author 48

NO ORDINARY DAY

October 9, 2012, began like any other day for Malala Yousafzai, a 15-year-old girl living in Swat, Pakistan. She woke up and went to school. She took an exam that day and thought she did well. She was happy as she began her ride home. She sat in the rear, near the open back of the truck that served as a school bus. Malala was chatting with her friends about the exam when they noticed two

Like kids across the world, students in the Swat Valley crowd onto buses to get to school.

young men standing in the road. The men waved at the bus to stop it, and one of them approached the driver. The other man came around to the back of the truck.

One of Malala's friends suggested they might be journalists. Perhaps they were there to talk to Malala. Ever since it had been revealed that Malala was the author of a popular blog, she had been interviewed by many journalists. On her blog, Malala had spoken up about the right of all girls to have an education. The Swat Valley had been controlled by a group called the Taliban as recently as three years earlier. The Taliban did not believe in educating girls. They believed that girls and women belonged

The Taliban

The majority of Pakistan's people are Muslim. Muslim people follow the religion of Islam. The Taliban is a small group of Muslim people who believe in an extreme interpretation of the Islamic system of laws called Sharia. The Taliban are extraordinarily conservative, believing that women and girls should not work, go to school, or even drive cars.

at home, taking care of their families. Speaking out against the Taliban was a dangerous thing to do. Malala looked around and noticed how quiet the street was. She wondered where all the people were and why a journalist would approach her on the bus.

School in Pakistan

The school that Malala attended was only for girls. This is common in Pakistan, where unmarried girls are not supposed to have contact with unrelated boys. The Swat Valley where Malala lived is especially conservative.

The man jumped onto the rear bumper of the bus and stared inside. "Who is Malala?" he shouted. No one answered. "Who is Malala?" he shouted again. None of the girls answered, but their eyes turned to look at Malala. She was the only one not wearing a veil over her face. Before Malala could say anything, the man raised a gun and fired it several times. He shot Malala and two nearby friends at close range.

Local residents rushed Malala to a hospital in Swat after the shooting

Surviving to Fight

Malala collapsed onto her friend's lap. Blood flowed from her face and ear. The girls on the bus began screaming, and the men ran off. The bus driver sped to the hospital. Malala had been shot in the head. Her two friends were wounded in their arms and shoulders. Miraculously, Malala and her friends survived their injuries.

The Taliban had tried to kill Malala. But instead of frightening her, they gave her strength. Instead of silencing her, Malala's attackers made her voice heard around the world.

Malala's first public speech after the shooting was on July 12, 2013, her sixteenth birthday. She addressed the United Nations (UN), an international organization that works to promote international cooperation:

> *I raise up my voice—not so that I can shout, but so that those without a voice can be heard. Those who have fought for their rights: Their right to live in peace. Their right to be treated with dignity. Their right to equality of opportunity. Their right to be educated. . . . The Taliban shot me. . . . They shot my friends too. They thought that the bullets would silence us. But they failed. And then, out of that silence came thousands of voices. The terrorists thought that they would change our aims and stop our ambitions, but nothing changed in my life except this: weakness, fear and hopelessness died. Strength, power, and courage was born.*
>
> *Source: "Malala Yousafzai Speech in Full." BBC News. BBC News, July 12, 2013. Web. Accessed July 29, 2014.*

What's the Big Idea?

Take a close look at this speech. What is Malala's main point about speaking up? What does she hope to achieve? Pick out two rights for which she is fighting. What can you tell about Malala's personality based on this speech?

CHAPTER TWO

BORN A POOR GIRL

Malala Yousafzai was born in Mingora, Pakistan, on July 12, 1997. Mingora is the largest town in Swat, a beautiful, green valley in the province of Khyber Pakhtunkhwa. Swat is generally known for being a highly religious and peaceful area. It had become popular among tourists from Pakistan and around the world. Before the Taliban took power in the 1990s, local residents

Decades ago, Swat was known for being a peaceful region.

Pakistan Map

This is a map of Pakistan and the surrounding region. What four countries share borders with Pakistan? Find the Swat Valley and the city of Mingora, where Malala lived. Which neighboring country is closest to Malala's home?

had enjoyed access to modern education and healthcare. Once it was in control, however, the Taliban shut down schools and restricted the rights of Swat's residents.

When Malala was born, her parents were very poor. They could not pay for the hospital or a midwife. Tor Pekai, Malala's mother, gave birth at home. Only a neighbor came to help her. Malala's home was a two-room shack. There was no bathroom, kitchen, or running water. Her mother cooked over a campfire.

Islam is the state religion of Pakistan. People who follow Islam are called Muslims. More than 95 percent of Pakistan's population is

Pakistan

Pakistan is a relatively new country. It was created in 1947 when British-controlled India was divided into two countries: Pakistan and India. Generally, Muslims settled in Pakistan, and Hindus, who follow the religion of Hinduism, settled in India. Wars between the two countries resulted in the splitting of Pakistan. Its eastern portion formed a third country, Bangladesh, in 1971. Pakistan and India continue to struggle for control of the Kashmir territory, an area located between Pakistan, India, and China. Pakistan's government and military also battle many armed rebel groups, such as the Taliban, within their own country.

Muslim. Traditionally Pakistan is a male-dominated society. Women are considered secondary to men. In many families, women still observe a custom called *purdah*. This is the physical separation of women from unrelated men. According to this custom, women stay at home and take care of the family. They rarely leave the house. If they do go out, they must cover their heads and faces with a veil called a burka. Because boys are usually more valued than girls, people celebrate the birth of a son. But when a daughter is born, they are often disappointed.

Free as a Bird

When Malala was born, her father wrote her name in the family tree for the Yousafzai clan. Malala was the first female to be listed in this important document. Her father said that he never wanted to clip her wings, so she could follow her dreams. He often said, "Malala is free as a bird."

Malala's Family

Malala's father, Ziauddin Yousafzai, was different from most Pakistani men. From the beginning, he adored Malala and treated

Students at Malala's school continued to attend classes even after the horrific shooting.

her like other fathers treated their sons. He asked his friends to throw coins, dried fruits, and candies into her cradle. Usually this is only done for boys.

Ziauddin owned a private school across the street from their shack. The school, named the Khushal School, taught boys and girls. When Malala was a few months old, the family moved into three rooms above the school. The apartment was small, but at least it had running water. As a toddler, Malala played in the

Malala's father had long been an advocate for education equality in Pakistan.

school. She wandered into classrooms and pretended to teach the students. Her father put her in classes when she was just three or four years old. The other students were much older than she was. But Malala didn't mind. She listened to the lessons and mimicked the teachers. Malala has said that she "grew up in a school."

By 2004 Malala had two younger brothers, Khushal and Atal. The school had more students, and her family was able to move into a bigger house. As Malala grew, so did her desire to help people. She learned by watching the way her parents treated others. Her mother visited the sick in hospitals, let many relatives live with them, and fed poor students breakfast before school. Her father allowed many children to attend his school for free. He taught poor families that their children deserved to go to school. Malala's father was also concerned about the environment. He started an organization to help people understand how to live peacefully and protect the environment in Swat. He taught Malala and her brothers that "if you help someone in need you might also receive unexpected aid."

CHAPTER THREE

BECOMING AN ACTIVIST

Malala's father has been a major influence in her life. He was educated at the prestigious Jehanzeb College in Swat. He firmly believed a lack of education was the source of Pakistan's problems. Because people were ignorant, they continued to elect dishonest leaders. Malala's father thought schooling should be provided for everybody, no matter how much money they had

Malala's interest in education and activism was inspired by her father.

The Scavenger Children

When Malala was nine, her mother sent her to the rubbish dump to throw some things away. There she saw young children collecting and sorting trash to sell. One girl was Malala's age. She was dirty and had sores all over her body. Malala realized how lucky she was. She did not have to work. She could go to school. Malala begged her father to give the scavenger children places at his school. This was the beginning of her fight for the rights of children to education.

or whether they were boys or girls. He opened his own school so he could teach children to think for themselves. He encouraged them to be creative and keep their minds open to new ideas. He passed these beliefs on to Malala.

Malala also became interested in politics through her father. He often had friends over to talk about local and national issues. Malala liked to sit next to him and listen to their discussions. The local government had become very conservative. Music and movies were banned. Some local leaders tried to shut down her father's school because they

believed girls should stay at home. After the Taliban rose to power in Swat in 2008, they continued to threaten Ziauddin. They also told all women in the area, including teachers and nurses, to stop working and remain in their homes.

Tragedy Strikes Pakistan

One of Malala's greatest role models was Benazir Bhutto, who lived from 1953 to 2007. Bhutto had been the first female prime minister of Pakistan. She showed Malala that girls could speak out and become government leaders. For Malala and many others, Bhutto was a symbol of hope and a return to a

A Bookish Girl

Malala has described herself as "a bookish girl." Her classmates said she was "a genius girl." She was very competitive academically. The first time she didn't earn the best grade in class, she cried. On special occasions, Pakistani girls draw temporary tattoos on their hands using henna. Instead of the traditional flowers and butterflies, Malala and her friends drew mathematical and chemical formulas to show off their knowledge.

democratic government. In December 2007, she was assassinated at a public rally. This horrible event inspired Malala to fight for women's rights.

After Bhutto's death, Malala felt a sense of hopelessness. She was not sure that the situation in her country would get better. Even though she had to hide her schoolbooks in her shawl, Malala kept going to school. There she felt safe from the terrors outside. Then the Taliban began bombing schools in Swat. They bombed at night, when schools were empty. Explosions in Mingora were close enough to make Malala's house shake.

A news reporter went to Mingora in November 2007. He went to interview Malala's father, who had been speaking out against the Taliban. While there, the reporter also spoke to Malala's class. Malala told him, "I'm very frightened. . . . Nowadays explosions are increasing. We can't sleep. Our siblings are terrified, and we cannot come to school." Malala's interview was shown on television that night across Pakistan. She was only ten years old.

EXPLORE ONLINE

The focus in Chapter Three is on the role of education in Malala's life. It also touches on the state of education in Pakistan. The website below focuses on Pakistan. Find the section on education. As you know, every source is different. How is the information given in the website different from the information in this chapter? What information is the same? How do the two sources present information differently?

Pakistan
www.mycorelibrary.com/malala-yousafzai

CHAPTER FOUR

BECOMING A TARGET

As Swat became more violent, Malala's father continued to work for peace. He gave many radio interviews and encouraged Malala to speak out too. Malala began to appear on radio and television shows in 2008. She talked about her rights and the rights of girls. She believed God wanted her to speak the truth. In September Malala gave a speech on a popular talk show. Her speech was titled

Taliban attacks reduced many schools to rubble.

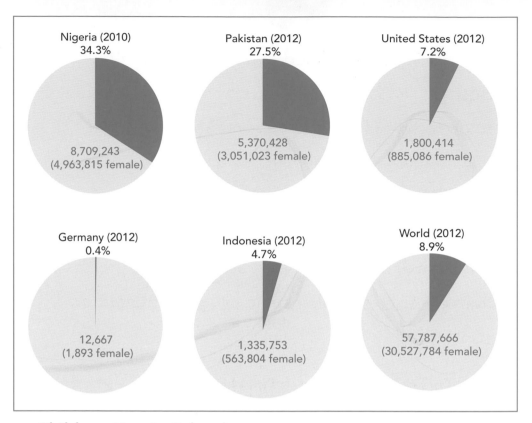

Children Not in School

This chart shows the number of children ages 6–11 who are not in school in selected countries in the world. Which country has the most children out of school? How does the number of children out of school in Pakistan compare to the other countries shown here? Are more boys or girls out of school?

"How dare the Taliban take away my basic right to education?" It was heard by many people. But the Taliban didn't stop blowing up schools. By December 2008, hundreds of schools had been destroyed.

The Taliban declared that all girls' schools must close on January 15, 2009. Girls would not be allowed to go to school anymore. At first Malala thought it was a joke. Then she became angry. She knew education was very important. By denying her an education, the Taliban was taking away her future. She told herself that though the Taliban could prevent her from going to school, it could not prevent her from thinking.

Malala and the Media

The violence in Swat increased. The Taliban hurt or killed people for doing things they judged to be against Sharia law. A reporter asked Malala's father to find a schoolgirl to write an online diary about life under the Taliban. Malala volunteered. She began writing in January 2009 under the name Gul Makai, which means "cornflower." Her blog shared details about her fears and nightmares. It also included information about her experiences in school. The blog was published on a popular news website and

On Courage

Malala has been praised for her bravery. She spoke up for girls' rights to education when it was very dangerous to do so. But that doesn't mean she is never afraid. At the We Day UK festival in March 2014, Malala said, "I have fears. I fear ghosts and dragons. But I have learned something long ago: Never let your fears get bigger than your courage. Your courage should always be stronger than your fear."

translated into English. It began to attract attention in other countries. Malala discovered words could have more power than the Taliban's guns.

In February, Malala appeared in a *New York Times* documentary about the ban on girls' education in Swat. In the video, Malala asks the world to help her country. After her school closed, Malala was crushed. She spoke out on radio and television shows. On her blog, she wrote about how the Pakistani army wasn't doing anything to stop the Taliban. Malala's voice was heard. People outside of Swat protested. Several weeks later, the Taliban lifted the ban, but only for girls up to ten years old. Malala was eleven, but she pretended to be younger and snuck back to school.

The Taliban continued to gain power in Swat. After many failed negotiations, the Pakistani army decided to battle the Taliban and drive them out of Swat. In early May 2009, nearly 2 million people fled Swat, including Malala and her family. Malala's family spent three months in exile in Islamabad, the nation's capital. They lived with friends and relatives. Their life became so chaotic that nobody remembered Malala's twelfth birthday. Even though she didn't have a cake or candles, Malala made a wish. She wished for peace. She continued to write her blog, which was now being read all over the world.

On the way back to Mingora in September, Malala saw ruined villages. Buildings had been blown up. Shops had been robbed and destroyed. Soldiers were everywhere. But the fighting had ended, and the Taliban had run away. Slowly people returned to their homes. Malala starred in another documentary

Residents of Mingora fled overnight before the Pakistani military arrived to fight the Taliban.

about escaping Swat and then returning home. The video was seen worldwide, and Malala's fame grew. In December 2009, she was revealed as being the author of her blog. Over the next two years, she continued to speak up for girls' education rights. In December 2011, Malala was awarded Pakistan's first National Youth Peace Prize. She won more awards and prizes from around the world. But she also became a target.

The Attack

People who speak out against the Taliban are often targeted. But Malala thought the group would ignore her because she was a child. In January 2012, Malala learned that the Taliban had issued threats directly against her. Malala was not worried. She felt death was something that could not be prevented. She decided not to keep quiet. But her mother insisted that Malala take the bus instead of walking home.

The Taliban found Malala anyway. On October 9, 2012, she was shot in the head on the school bus. She was very lucky. The bullet did not

Malala's Friends

Two of Malala's friends, Kainat Riaz and Shazia Ramzan, were also shot on the bus. Both recovered from their injuries and returned to the Khushal School to continue their education, even though it was risky. In July 2013, both Kainat and Shazia were offered scholarships to attend Atlantic College, an international school located in Wales in the United Kingdom. They are now studying at the school and are determined to continue their education.

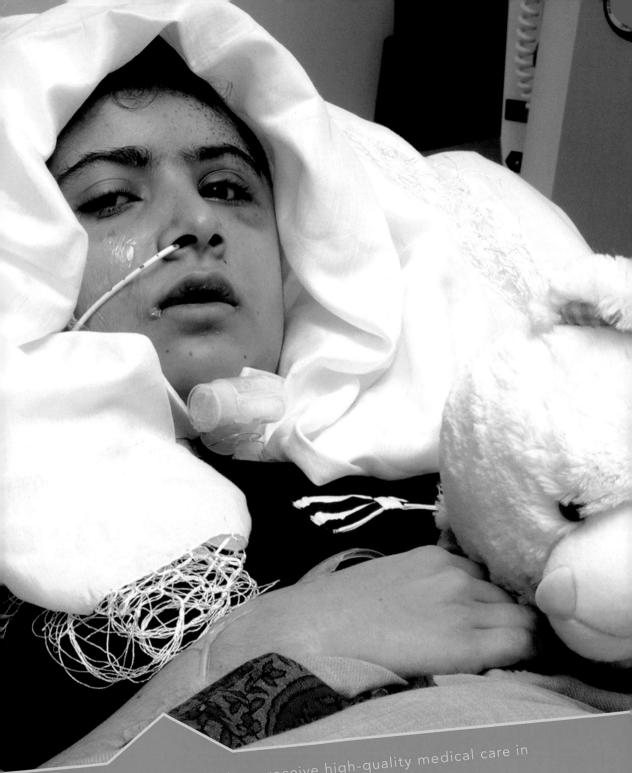

Malala was able to receive high-quality medical care in the United Kingdom.

enter her brain. However, bone splinters caused her brain to swell. The bullet also damaged her left ear and the nerves in her face. Despite several surgeries, her health became worse. She was flown to England to receive additional care. Malala made an amazing recovery. Determined not to miss more school, she started going to high school in England in March 2013, only five months after being shot.

FURTHER EVIDENCE

There is a lot of information about Malala's activism in Chapter Four. The chapter also discusses the actions of the Taliban. What is one of the main points of this chapter? What are some pieces of evidence in the chapter that support this main point? Go to the article about Malala at the website below. Find a quote from the article that supports the chapter's main point. Does the quote match an existing piece of evidence in the chapter? Or does it add a new one?

An Attack in Pakistan
www.mycorelibrary.com/malala-yousafzai

CHAPTER FIVE

THE WORLD LISTENS TO MALALA

Millions of people all over the world were shocked by Malala's shooting. Government leaders, politicians, and celebrities rushed to support her campaign. Former British Prime Minister Gordon Brown started a petition with the slogan, "I am Malala." The petition called for education to be provided for every child by 2015.

In the days following the attack, protesters in Pakistan stood in solidarity with Malala.

Malala's appearance at the United Nations drew cheers from the hundreds of young people in the audience.

With more than 1 million signatures, the petition helped to change Pakistan's education policy.

Pakistan's government later passed a Right to Education bill, the first one in the country's history. Now poor families will receive a small payment for each child who goes to elementary school. In December 2012, Pakistani president Asif Ali Zardari announced the establishment of a $10 million education fund in Malala's name.

Making an Impact

On her sixteenth birthday in 2013, Malala spoke at the United Nations in front of a special youth assembly. It was her first public speech since the shooting. Her words helped draw attention to the UN Global Education First Initiative. One of the goals of this program is to put every child in school by 2015. More than $1.5 billion has been pledged for the initiative so far.

Before the shooting, Malala had wanted to start an education foundation. She was finally able to achieve this goal with the creation of the Malala Fund. The fund has already given $45,000 to 40 girls in Swat to go to

Malala Day

The United Nations declared Malala's sixteenth birthday, July 12, 2013, to be Malala Day. On that day, Malala delivered to the UN a set of education demands written by young people. Youth leaders around the world gathered together and voiced their support for the UN Global Education First Initiative. This program works to make sure that all children, especially girls, are in school and getting an education.

school. Now these girls will not have to compete with their brothers for family resources to attend classes.

Malala has won many awards, including the United Nations Human Rights Prize and the Nobel Peace Prize.

Malala has become a symbol of equal rights for women and educational rights for all children. She has inspired young people to speak up. In Pakistan, girls wear headbands and shirts that say, "I am Malala." They show their support for Malala's cause and demand change. In October 2013, she released a book cowritten

The Nobel Peace Prize

Each year, a committee appointed by the Norwegian Parliament awards the Nobel Peace Prize to a person who has contributed to world peace. In October 2014, the committee announced that Malala had won the 2014 prize, along with Indian child labor activist Kailash Satyarthi. Malala became the youngest winner in the prize's history. After announcing the award, the committee's chairman said, "Through her heroic struggle, she has become a leading spokesperson for girls' rights to education."

After the release of her memoir, Malala met with Queen Elizabeth II of the United Kingdom and gave her a copy of the book.

Malala participated in a ceremony to open a new public library in Birmingham in late 2013.

with British journalist Christina Lamb called *I Am Malala*. The book detailed the attack, discussed the aftermath, and shared Malala's thoughts on education.

Malala lives in England now. She attends high school in the city of Birmingham. She misses Mingora, but it is not safe for her to return home. The Taliban has said they will attack her again if given the chance. She is in exile once more. For now, Malala continues to fight for change with her books, her pen, and her voice. One day she hopes she will be the prime minister of Pakistan.

Malala concluded her July 12, 2013, speech at the United Nations by saying:

> *We must not forget that millions of people are suffering from poverty, injustice and ignorance. We must not forget that millions of children are out of schools. We must not forget that our sisters and brothers are waiting for a bright, peaceful future. So let us wage a global struggle against illiteracy, poverty and terrorism and let us pick up our books and pens. They are our most powerful weapons. One child, one teacher, one pen and one book can change the world. Education is the only solution. Education first.*
>
> Source: "Malala Yousafzai Speech in Full." BBC News. BBC News, July 12, 2013. Web. Accessed July 29, 2014.

Changing Minds

Take a position on the power of books and pens to change the world. Imagine that your best friend doesn't believe education is a powerful force for change. Write an editorial trying to change your friend's mind. Make sure you explain your opinion and your reasons for it. Include facts and details that support your opinion.

IMPORTANT DATES

1997

Malala Yousafzai is born in Mingora, Pakistan, on July 12.

2008

At the age of 11, Malala gives her first public speech, called "How dare the Taliban take away my basic right to education?"

2009

In January Malala begins blogging about life as a schoolgirl under Taliban rule.

2009

In September Malala and her family, along with hundreds of thousands of other displaced people, return to Swat.

2011

In December Malala wins Pakistan's National Youth Peace Prize, and her identity as a blogger is revealed.

2012

On October 9 Malala and two friends are shot by a Taliban gunman on their way home from school.

2009

On January 15 the Taliban prohibits girls from attending school and forces Malala's father to close his school.

2009

The New York Times releases a documentary featuring Malala in February.

2009

In May Malala and her family flee the conflict in Swat between the Pakistani army and the Taliban.

2013

On her sixteenth birthday, Malala speaks at the United Nations about children's rights to education.

2013

Malala's autobiography is released in October.

2014

In October Malala wins the Nobel Peace Prize.

Say What?

Studying a different culture can mean learning a lot of new vocabulary. Find five words in this book that you've never heard before. Use a dictionary to find out what they mean. Write the meanings in your own words, and use each new word in a sentence.

You Are There

This book discusses what it is like to live in Pakistan under the rule of the Taliban. Imagine that you are a girl or boy living in the Swat Valley in Pakistan. The Taliban rebels have just arrived in your village to try to convince you to fight against the Pakistani government and to follow a strict version of Islamic law. Write a short story about your reaction to these events. Do you believe the Taliban should take over the country? How do your parents and village leaders feel?

Surprise Me

Chapter Two discusses the treatment of women in Pakistan. After reading this book, what two or three facts about women's roles in Pakistan did you find most surprising? Write a few sentences about each fact. Why did you find them surprising?

Take a Stand

Do you think Malala should have agreed to write a blog and to give public speeches? Or should she have refused to do so for her own safety? Write a short essay explaining your opinion. Make sure to give reasons for your opinion, along with supporting facts and details.

GLOSSARY

conservative
wanting to preserve existing conditions and traditional views

documentary
a factual film or television program

exile
being forced to leave one's home or country

foundation
an organization that collects and provides funds for a cause

henna
a reddish-brown dye obtained from a plant and often used to create temporary tattoos

Islam
a religion whose followers believe in one god who has revealed himself through a prophet named Muhammad, born in the 500s CE

journalist
a person who writes and produces news stories

midwife
a person who helps during childbirth

petition
a written request signed by supporters

prime minister
a leader of a political party serving as the head of a government

LEARN MORE

Books

Sonneborn, Liz. *Pakistan*. New York: Children's Press, 2013.

Yousafzai, Malala. *I am Malala: How One Girl Stood Up for Education and Changed the World*. New York: Little, Brown Books for Young Readers, 2014.

Websites

To learn more about Newsmakers, visit **booklinks.abdopublishing.com**. These links are routinely monitored and updated to provide the most current information available.

Visit **www.mycorelibrary.com** for free additional tools for teachers and students.

INDEX

awards, 30, 38

Bhutto, Benazir, 21–22
Birmingham, England, 40
blog, 6, 27–30
book, 38–40

family, 13–17
friends, 6–8, 22, 31

Islam, 6, 13

journalists, 6, 23, 27–28, 40

Malala Fund, 37
Mingora, Pakistan, 11–12, 22–23, 29, 40

Pakistan, 6, 7, 12–13, 21, 26

recovery, 33

schools, 5, 7, 15–17, 20, 22, 26, 27, 33, 37–38
shooting, 7–8, 31–33
Swat, Pakistan, 5–7, 11–12, 17, 19, 21–22, 25, 27–30, 37

Taliban, 6–9, 11–12, 21–23, 26–29, 31, 33, 40

United Nations, 9, 37, 41

Yousafzai, Ziauddin, 14–15, 19–21, 23, 25, 27

ABOUT THE AUTHOR

Andrea Wang was an environmental scientist before becoming an author. She lives in the Boston area with her husband and two children.